How to be
Filled with the
Holy Spirit

A. W. Tozer

GLH Publishing
Louisville, KY

Originally Published 1952, Public Domain

ISBN:
  Paperback 978-1-941129-84-5
  Epub 978-1-941129-85-2

CONTENTS

Preface

The following pages represent the gist of a series of sermons given on successive Sunday evenings to the congregation of the church of which I am pastor. The talks were taken down stenographically and later reduced to their present length. A fifth message which was a part of the series has been omitted here.

The fact that these were originally spoken messages accounts for their racy style and for the personal references which occur in them occasionally. Had I been writing the messages I should have exercised greater care in the composition. The subject is, however, so vitally important that I feel sure the reader will pardon the offhand style of the language. The truth is always good even when the vehicle in which it rides is homely and plain.

This book is made available to the Christian public with the prayer that it may help to lead many thirsty believers to the fountain of living waters.

—A. W. T.

I. Who is the Holy Spirit?

We all use the word "spirit" a great deal. Now I want to tell you what I do and do not mean by it. In the first place, we rule out all of the secondary uses of the word "spirit." I do not mean courage, as when we say, "That's the spirit!" I don't mean temper or temperament or pluck. I mean nothing so nebulous as that. Spirit is a specific and identifiable substance. If not definable, it can at least be described. Spirit is as real as matter, but it is another mode of being than matter.

We are all materialists to some extent. We are born of material parents into a material world; we are wrapped in material clothes and fed on material milk and lie in a material bed, and sleep and walk and live and talk and grow up in a world of matter. Matter presses upon us obtrusively and takes over our thinking so completely that we cannot speak of spirit without using materialistic terms. God made man out of the dust of the ground, and man has been dust ever since, and we can't quite shake it off.

Matter is one mode of being; spirit is another mode of being as authentic as matter.

Material things have certain characteristics. For instance, they have weight. Everything that is material weighs something; it yields to gravitational pull. Then, matter has dimensions; you can measure the thing if it is made of matter. It has shape. It has an outline of some sort, no matter whether it is a molecule or an atom or whatever it may be, on up to the stars that shine. Then, it is extended in space. So I say that weight, dimension, shape and extension are the things that belong to matter. That is one mode of being; that is one way of existing.

One power of spirit, of any spirit (for I am talking about spirit now, not about the Holy Spirit), is its ability to penetrate. Matter bumps against other matter and stops; it cannot penetrate. Spirit can penetrate everything. For instance, your body is made of matter, and yet your spirit has penetrated your body completely. Spirit can penetrate spirit. It can penetrate personality—oh, if God's people could only learn that spirit can penetrate personality, that your personality is not an impenetrable substance, but can be penetrated. A mind can be penetrated by thought, and the air can be penetrated by light, and material things and mental things, and even spiritual things, can be penetrated by spirit.

What is the Holy Spirit?

Now, what is the Holy Spirit? Not who, but what? The answer is that the Holy Spirit is a Being dwelling in another mode of existence. He has not weight, nor measure, nor size, nor any color, no extension in space, but He nevertheless exists as surely as you exist.

The Holy Spirit is not enthusiasm. I have found enthusiasm that hummed with excitement, and the Holy Spirit was nowhere to be found there at all; and I have found the Holy Ghost when there has not been much of what we call enthusiasm present. Neither is the Holy Spirit another name for genius. We talk about the spirit of Beethoven and say, "This or that artist played with great spirit." The Holy Spirit is none of these things. Now what is He?

He is a Person. Put that down in capital letters—that the Holy Spirit is not only a Being having another mode of existence, but He is Himself a Person, with all the qualities and powers of personality. He is not matter, but He is substance. The Holy Spirit is often thought of as a beneficent wind that blows across the Church.

If you think of the Holy Spirit as being literally a wind, a breath, then you think of Him as nonpersonal and nonindividual. But the Holy Spirit has will and intelligence and feeling and knowledge and sympathy and ability to love and see and think and hear and speak and desire the same as any person has.

You may say, "I believe all that. You surely don't think you are telling us anything new!" I don't hope to tell you very much that is new; I only hope to set the table for you, arranging the dishes a little better and a little more attractively so that you will be tempted to partake. Many of us have grown up on the theology that accepts the Holy Spirit as a Person, and even as a divine Person, but for some reason it never did us any good. We are as empty as ever, we are as joyless as ever, we are as far from peace as ever, we are as weak as ever. What I want to do is to tell you the old things, but while I am doing it, to encourage your heart to make them yours now, and to walk into the living, throbbing, vibrating heart of them, so that from here on your life will be altogether different.

Who is the Holy Spirit?

So the Spirit is a Person. That's what He is. Now who is He?

What the Creeds Say

The historic church has said that He is God. Let me quote from the Nicene Creed: "I believe in the Holy Ghost, the Lord and Giver of life, Which proceedeth from the Father and the Son, and with the Father and the Son together is worshiped and glorified."

That is what the Church believed about the Holy Ghost 1,600 years ago. Let's be daring for a moment. Let's try to think away this idea that the Holy Spirit is truly God. All right. Let's admit something else into the picture. Let's say, "I believe in one Holy Ghost, the Lord and Giver of life, who with the Father and the Son is to be worshiped and glorified." For the "Holy Ghost," let's put in "Abraham, the father of the faithful, who with the Father and the Son together is worshiped and glorified." That is a monstrous thing, and in your heart already there is a shocked feeling. You couldn't do it. You couldn't admit a mere man into the holy circle of the Trinity! The Father and Son are to be worshiped and glorified, and if the Holy Spirit is to be included here He has to be equal to the Father and the Son.

Now let's look at the Athanasian Creed. Thirteen hundred years old it is. Notice what it says about the Holy Spirit: "Such as the Father is, such is the Son, and such is the Holy Ghost." Once more let's do that terrible thing. Let's introduce into this concept the name of a man. Let's put David in there. Let's say, "Such as the Father is, so also is the Son, and such is the hymnist David." That would be a shock like cold water in the face! You can't do that. And you can't put the archangel Michael in there. You can't say, "Such as the Father is, such also is the Son, and such is the archangel Michael." That would be monstrous inconsistency, and you know it!

I have told you what the creeds of the church say. If the Bible is taught otherwise, I would throw the creeds away. Nobody can come down the years with flowing beard, and with the dust of centuries upon him, and get me to believe a doctrine unless he can give me chapter and verse. I quote the creeds, but I preach them only so far as they summarize the teachings of the Bible on a given subject. If there were any divergency from the teachings of the Word of God I would not teach the creed; I would teach the Book, for the Book is the source of all authentic information. However, our fathers did a mighty good job of going into the Bible, finding out what it taught, and then formulating the creeds for us.

What the Hymnists Say

Now let's look at what our songwriters and our hymnists believed. Recall the words the quartet sang this evening:

> Holy Ghost, with light divine,
> Shine upon this heart of mine.

Let's pray that prayer to Gabriel, to Saint Bernard, to D. L. Moody. Let's pray that prayer to any man or creature that has ever served God. You can't pray that kind of prayer to a creature. To put those words into a

hymn means that the one about whom you are speak-
ing must be God.

> Holy Ghost, with power divine,
> Cleanse this guilty heart of mine.

Who can get into the intricate depths of a human
soul, into the deep confines of a human spirit and cleanse
it? Nobody but the God who made it! The hymn writer
who said "Cleanse this guilty heart of mine" meant that
the Holy Ghost to whom he prayed was God.

> Holy Spirit, all divine,
> Dwell within this heart of mine;
> Cast down every idol throne;
> Reign supreme—and reign alone.

The church has sung that now for about one hun-
dred years. "Reign supreme—and reign alone." Could
you pray that to anybody you know? The man who
wrote that hymn believed that the Holy Ghost was God,
otherwise he wouldn't have said, "Reign supreme, and
reign all by Yourself." That is an invitation no man can
make to anybody, except the Divine One, except God.

What the Scriptures Say

Now the Scriptures. Notice that I am trying to establish
the truth that the Holy Spirit is not only a Person, but
that He is a divine Person; not only a divine Person, but
God.

In Psalm 139 the hymnist attributes omnipresence
to the Holy Ghost. He says, "Whither shall I go from
thy spirit? or whither shall I flee from thy presence?"
(139:7) and he develops throughout the 139th Psalm, in
language that is as beautiful as a sunrise and as musi-
cal as the wind through the willows, the idea that the
Spirit is everywhere, having the attributes of deity. He
must be deity, for no creature could have the attributes
of deity.

In Hebrews there is attributed to the Holy Ghost
that which is never attributed to an archangel, or a ser-
aphim, or a cherubim, or an angel, or an apostle, or a

martyr, or a prophet, or a patriarch, or anyone that has ever been created by the hand of God. It says, "through the eternal Spirit" (Hebrews 9:14), and every theologian knows that eternity is an attribute of no creature which deity has ever formed. The angels are not eternal; that is, they had a beginning, and all created things had a beginning. As soon as the word "eternal" is used about being it immediately establishes the fact that he never had a beginning, is not a creature at all, but God. Therefore, when the Holy Ghost says "the eternal Spirit" about Himself He is calling Himself God.

Again, the baptismal formula in Matthew 28:19 says, "baptizing them in the name of the Father, and of the Son, and of the Holy Ghost." Now try to imagine putting the name of a man in there: "baptizing them in the name of the Father, and of the Son, and of the Apostle Paul." You couldn't think it! It is horrible to contemplate! No man can be admitted into that closed circle of deity. We baptize in the name of the Father and the Son, because in the Son is equal with the Father in His Godhead, and we baptize in the name of the Holy Ghost because the Holy Ghost is also equal with the Father and the Son.

You say, "You are just a Trinitarian and we are Trinitarians already." Yes, I know it, but once again I tell you that I am trying to throw emphasis upon this teaching.

How many blessed truths have gotten snowed under. People believe them, but they are just not being taught, that is all. Here was a man and his wife, a very fine intelligent couple from another city. They named the church to which they belonged, and I instantly said, "That is a fine church!"

"Oh, yes," they said, "but they don't teach what we came over here for." They came over because they were ill and wanted to be scripturally anointed for healing. So I got together two missionaries, two preachers and an elder, and we anointed them and prayed for them. If you were to go to that church where they attended and say to the preacher, "Do you believe that the Lord answers prayer and heals the sick?" he would reply, "Sure, I do!" He believes it, but he doesn't teach it, and what you don't believe strongly enough to teach doesn't do you any good.

It is the same with the fullness of the Holy Ghost. Evangelical Christianity believes it, but nobody experiences it. It lies under the snow, forgotten. I am praying that God may be able to melt away the ice from this blessed truth, and let it spring up alive again, that the Church and the people who hear may get some good out of it and not merely say, "I believe" while it is buried under the snow of inactivity and non-attention.

Let us recapitulate. Who is the Spirit? The Spirit is God, existing in another mode of being than ourselves. He exists as a spirit and not as matter, for He is not matter, but He is God. He is a Person. It was so believed by the whole Church of Christ down through the years. It was so sung by the hymnists back in the days of the first hymn writers. It is so taught in the Book, all through the Old Testament and the New, and I have given you only a few proof texts. I could spend the evening reading Scripture stating this same thing.

What is He Like?

Now what follows from all this? Ah, there is an unseen Deity present, a knowing, feeling Personality, and He is indivisible from the Father and the Son, so that if you were to be suddenly transferred to heaven itself you wouldn't be any closer to God than you are now, for God is already here. Changing your geographical location would not bring you any nearer to God nor God any nearer to you, because the indivisible Trinity is present, and all that the Son is the Holy Ghost is, and all that the Father is the Holy Ghost is, and the Holy Ghost is in His Church.

What will we find Him to be like? He will be exactly like Jesus. You have read your New Testament, and you know what Jesus is like, and the Holy Spirit is exactly like Jesus, for Jesus was God and the Spirit is God, and the Father is exactly like the Son; and you can know what Jesus is like by knowing what the Father is like, and you can know what the Spirit is like by knowing what Jesus is like.

If Jesus were to come walking down this aisle there would be no stampede for the door. Nobody would scream and be frightened. We might begin to weep for sheer joy and delight that He had so honored us, but nobody would be afraid of Jesus; no mother with a little crying babe would ever have to be afraid of Jesus; no poor harlot being dragged by the hair of her head had to be afraid of Jesus—nobody! Nobody ever had to be afraid of Jesus, because He is the epitome of love, kindliness, geniality, warm attractiveness and sweetness. And that is exactly what the Holy Ghost is, for He is the Spirit of the Father and the Son. Amen.

II. The Promise of the Father

*And, behold, I send the promise of my Father upon
you: but tarry ye in the city of Jerusalem, until ye be
endued with power from on high.*
Luke 24:49

I wonder if you have ever thought of the origin of the
phrase Jesus used here. Why did He call it the Father's
promise? He didn't say "mine." He said, "The promise
of my Father." This takes us back to Joel 2:28–29:

> And it shall come to pass afterward, that I will pour
> out my spirit upon all flesh; and your sons and your
> daughters shall prophesy, your old men shall dream
> dreams, your young men shall see visions: and also
> upon the servants and upon the handmaids in those
> days will I pour out my spirit.

Now, when our Lord Jesus came He authoritative-
ly interpreted this, and tied up His intention for His
Church with the ancient promises given by the Father
centuries before.

In fulfillment of all this there were three periods
discernible in the New Testament: (1) The period of the
promise, (2) the period of the preparation and (3) the
period of the realization—all this having to do with the
promise of the Father and the intention of the Son to-
ward His people.

The Period of the Promise

The period of the promise extends from John the Bap-
tist, roughly, to the resurrection of our Lord Jesus. The
marks of it are these: that there were disciples, and they
were commissioned and instructed, and they exercised
their commission and the authority granted them by

the Lord. They knew the Lord Jesus; they loved Him. They knew Him living, they knew Him and saw Him dead, and they saw Him risen again from the dead. All the time our Lord was with them. He was busy creating expectation in them. He was telling His disciples that in spite of all they had and all the blessing that God the Father had given them, they were still to expect the coming of a new and superior kind of life. He was creating an expectation of an effusion of outpoured energy which they, at their best, did not yet enjoy.

The Period of the Preparation

Then our Lord rose from the dead and we have what we call the period of the preparation. That was the short period of the preparation. That was the short period which intervened between our Lord's resurrection and the down-coming of the Holy Ghost. They had stopped their activity at the specific command of the Lord. He said, "Tarry! You are about to receive that which has been promised. Your expectations are about to be fulfilled, your hopes realized. Therefore, don't do anything until it comes."

I might say here that sometimes you are going farther when you are not going anywhere; you are moving faster when you are not moving at all; you are learning more when you think you have stopped learning. These disciples had reached an impasse. Their Lord had risen, and they had seen Him, and with excitement and joy they knew He had risen from the dead. Now He had gone from them. Where was He? They gathered together, as you and I might have done under like circumstances, waiting, all of one accord. That is more than they had done during the period of the promise. But here were 120 of them, and they had a oneness of accord.

The Period of the Realization

The period of realization came upon them when the Father fulfilled His promise and sent the Spirit. Peter used a phrase to describe it which is one of the fullest, finest phrases I know. He said, "He hath shed forth this, which ye now see and hear" (Acts 2:33)—the shedding forth was like a mighty down-coming of water. The expectations were more than met—not fully met, but more than met. God always gives us an overplus. They got more than they expected.

Now what happened here? What did they receive that they had not had before? Well, first, they had a new kind of evidence for the reality of their faith. You see, Christ talked about four lines of evidence of His Messiahship.

He said, "Search the scriptures; for in them ye think ye have eternal life: and they are they which testify of me" (John 5:39). The Scriptures were proof of who Christ was. That is one line of evidence.

Another line is the witness of John the Baptist who pointed to Jesus and said, "Behold the Lamb of God, which taketh away the sin of the world" (1:29).

Jesus gives us another line of evidence. He said, "The Father himself...hath borne witness of me" (5:37), and there was a third proof of His Messiahship, and authentic proof of it.

He gave a fourth. He said, "The same works that I do, bear witness of me, that the Father hath sent me.... Believe me for the very works' sake" (5:36; 14:11).

Have you noticed there is one serious breakdown there, a breakdown which our Lord recognized and which He remedied when the Holy Spirit came? That breakdown lies in the necessary externality of the proof. In every instance the proofs which our Lord adduced to His own Messiahship were external to the individual. They are not inside of the man. He has to open the Book and read. That is external to the man.

When I hear that the Church of Christ has gone throughout the whole world carrying the torch of civilization, healing and giving hope and help, I conclude the Christian Church must be of God because she is acting the way God would act. When I hear that she has founded hospitals and insane asylums, I say surely she must be of God because that is what God would do, being what He is. When I hear that she has eman-cipated woman and has taken her from being a chattel slave and an object of some old king's lust to being the equal of the man and queen in his home, I say surely that must be of God.

You can go down the corridors of history, and you can adduce proof of the divinity of the Church from what the Church has done. You can show how she brought civilization here and she brought help there. She cleaned up saloons in this town, and she delivered this young fellow from drink. We say that must be God. But that is external proof and it depends upon logic.

The Internal Evidence

There is another kind of evidence. It is the immediate evidence of the inner life. That is the evidence by which you know you are alive. If I were to prove that you weren't alive, you would chuckle and go home just as alive as you are now and not be a bit worried about it, because you have the instant, unmediated evidence of internal life.

Jesus Christ wanted to take religion out of the ex-ternal and make it internal and put it on the same level as life itself, so that a man knows he knows God the same as he knows he is himself and not somebody else. He knows he knows God the same as he knows he is alive and not dead. Only the Holy Ghost can do that. The Holy Spirit came to carry the evidence of Christian-ity from the books of apologetics into the human heart, and that is exactly what He does.

You can take the gospel of Jesus Christ to the hea-then in Borneo, or Africa, people who could never con-ceive the first premise of your logical arguments, so that it would be totally impossible for them to decide on logical grounds whether Christianity was of God or not. Preach Christ to them and they will believe and be transformed and put away their wickedness and change from evil to righteousness and get happy about it all, learn to read and write and study their Bibles and become leaders and pillars in their own church, transformed and made over. How? By the instant witness of the Holy Ghost to their hearts. This is the new thing that came, sir! God took religion from the realm of the external and made it internal.

Our trouble is that we are trying to confirm the truth of Christianity by an appeal to external evidence. We are saying, "Well, look at this fellow. He can throw a baseball farther than anybody else and he is a Christian, therefore Christianity must be true." "Here is a great statesman who believes the Bible. Therefore, the Bible must be true." We quote Daniel Webster or Roger Bacon. We write books to show that some scientist believed in Christianity: therefore, Christianity must be true.

We are all the way out on the wrong track, brother! That is not New Testament Christianity at all. That is a pitiful, whimpering, drooling appeal to the flesh. That never was the testimony of the New Testament, never the way God did things—never! You might satisfy the intellects of men by external evidences, and Christ did, I say, point to external evidence when He was here on earth.

The Witness of the Holy Spirit

But He said, "I am sending you something better. I am taking Christian apologetics out of the realm of logic and putting it into the realm of life. I am proving My deity, and My proof will not be an appeal to a general or a prime minister. The proof lies in an invisible, unseen but powerful energy that visits the human soul when the gospel is preached—the Holy Ghost!"

The Spirit of the living God brought an evidence that needed no logic; it went straight to the soul like a flash of silver light, like the direct plunge of a sharp spear into the heart. Those are the very words that Scripture uses when it says "pierced (pricked) to the heart." One translator points out that that word "pricked" is a word that means that it goes in deeper than the spear that pierced Jesus' side!

That is the way God does. There is an immediate

witness, an unmeditated push of the Spirit of God upon the spirit of man. There is a filtering down, a getting down into the very cells of that human soul and the impression on that soul by the Holy Ghost that this is true. That is what those disciples had never had before, and that is exactly what the Church does not have now. That is what we fundamentalist preachers wish we had and don't have, and that is why we are going so far astray to prove things. That, incidentally, is why this humble pulpit is never open to a man who wants to prove Christianity by means of appeal to external evidence. You can't do it to begin with, and I wouldn't do it to end with. We have something better.

Then, also, the Spirit gave a bright, emotional quality to their religion, and I grieve before my God over the lack of this in our day. The emotional quality isn't there. There is a sickliness about us all; we pump so hard trying to get a little drop of delight out of our old rusty well, and we write innumerable bouncy choruses, and we pump and pump until you could hear the old rusty thing squeak across forty acres. But it doesn't work.

Then He gave them direct spiritual authority. By that I mean He removed their fears, their questions, their apologies and their doubts, and they had an authority that was founded upon life.

The Spirit comes Today

There is a great modern error which I want to mention: it is that the coming of the Spirit happened once and for all, that the individual Christian is not affected by it. It is like the birth of Christ which happened once and for all and the most excellent sermon on the birth of Christ would never have that birth repeated, and all the prayers in the wide world would never have Christ born again of the Virgin Mary.

It is, they say, like the death and resurrection of Christ—never to be repeated. This error asserts that the coming of the Holy Spirit is an historic thing, an advance in the dispensational workings of God; but that it is all settled now and we need give no further thought

16

A. W. Tozer

to it. It is all here and we have it all, and if we believe in Christ that is it and there isn't anything more.

All right. Now everybody has a right to his view, if he thinks it is scriptural; but I would just like to ask some questions. I won't answer them; I'll just ask them, and you preach your own sermon.

Is the promise of the Father, with all its attendant riches of spiritual grace and power, intended to be for the first-century Christians only? Does the new birth, which the first-century Christians had to have, suffice for all other Christians, or is the new birth which they had to have that which we have to have? Does the new birth have to be repeated in each Christian before it is valid, or did that first church get born again for us? Can you get born again by proxy? The fact that those first 120 were born again, does that mean that we don't have to be? Now you answer me.

You say, "No, certainly we agree that everybody has to have the new birth for himself, individually." All right, if that is true (and it is), is the fullness of the Spirit which those first Christians received enough? Does that work for you and me? They had the fullness; now they are dead. Does the fact that they were filled avail to me? You answer that question.

Again, I want to ask you, would a meal eaten by Saint Peter in the year A.D. 33 nourish me today? Would a good meal of barley cakes and milk, and honey spread on the barley cake—a good meal for a good Jew in Peter's day—nourish me today? No, Peter is dead, and I can't be nourished by what Peter ate.

Would the fullness of the Holy Ghost that Peter got in the upper chamber do for me today, or must I receive individually what Peter received?

What value would the fullness of the Spirit in the church in Jerusalem have for us today if it was done over there once for all and we can't have the same thing here? We are separated by 5,000 miles of water and by 2,000 years of time. Now what, that happened to them, can possibly avail to us?

I want to ask you some more questions: Do you see

any similarity between the average one of us Christians buzzing around Chicago and those apostles? Are you ready to believe that we have just what they had, and that every believer in Chicago who accepts the Bible and is converted immediately enters into and now enjoys and possesses exactly what they did back there? Surely you know better than that!

This modern fundamentalism as we know it and of which we are a part—is it a satisfactory fulfillment of the expectations raised by the Father and Christ? Our Father who is in heaven raised certain high expectations of what He was going to do for His redeemed people. When His Son came to redeem those people, He heightened those expectations, raised them, clarified them, extended them, enlarged them and emphasized them. He raised an expectation that was simply beyond words, too wonderful and beautiful and thrilling to imagine. I want to ask you: Is this level of Christianity which we fundamentalists in this city now enjoy what He meant by what He said?

Listen, brother. Our Lord Jesus Christ advertised that He was going away to the Father and He was going to send back for His people a wonderful gift, and He said, "Stay right here until it comes, because it will be the difference between failure and success to you."

Then the Spirit came. Was He equal to the advertising? Did they say, "Is this all He meant! Oh, it is disappointing!" No. The Scripture says they wondered. The word "wonder" is in their mouths and hearts. He gave so much more than He promised, because words were the promise and the Holy Ghost was the fulfillment.

The simple fact is that we believers are not up to what He gave us reason to expect. The only honest thing to do is admit this and do something about it. There certainly has been a vast breakdown somewhere between promise and fulfillment. That breakdown is not with our heavenly Father, for He always gives more than He promises.

Now I am going to ask that you reverently ponder this and set aside time and search the Scriptures, pray and yield, obey and believe, and see whether that which our Lord gave us reason to think could be the possession of the Church may not be ours in actual fulfillment and realization.

III. How to be filled with the Holy Spirit

Before we deal with the question of how to be filled with the Holy Spirit, there are some matters which first have to be settled. As believers you have to get them out of the way, and right here is where the difficulty arises. I have been afraid that my listeners might have gotten the idea somewhere that I had a how-to-be-filled-with-the-Spirit-in-five-easy-lessons doctrine, which I could give you. If you can have any such vague ideas as that, I can only stand before you and say, "I am sorry"; because it isn't true; I can't give you such a course. There are some things, I say, that you have to get out of the way, settled. One of them is: Before you are filled with the Holy Spirit you must be sure that you can be filled.

Is the Spirit-Filled Life for You?

Satan has opposed the doctrine of the Spirit-filled life about as bitterly as any other doctrine there is. He has confused it, opposed it, surrounded it with false notions and fears. He has blocked every effort of the Church of Christ to receive from the Father her divine and blood-bought patrimony. The Church has tragically neglected this great liberating truth—that there is now for the child of God a full and wonderful and completely satisfying anointing with the Holy Ghost.

So you have to be sure that it is for you. You must be sure that it is God's will for you; that is, that it is part of the total plan, that it is included and embraced within the work of Christ in redemption; that it is, as the old camp-meeting, praying folks used to say, "the purchase of His blood."

19

I might throw a bracket in here and say that when-
ever I use the neutral pronoun "it" I am talking about
the gift. When I speak directly of the Holy Spirit, I shall
use a personal pronoun, He or Him or His, referring
to a person, for the Holy Spirit is not an it, but the gift
of the Holy Spirit must necessarily in our English lan-
guage be called "it."

Can you Believe this is Part of God's Plan?

You must, I say, be satisfied that this is nothing added
or extra. The Spirit-filled life is not a special, deluxe edi-
tion of Christianity. It is part and parcel of the total plan
of God for His people.

You must be satisfied that it is not abnormal. I ad-
mit that it is unusual, because there are so few people
who walk in the light of it or enjoy it, but it is not ab-
normal. In a world where everybody was sick, health
would be unusual, but it wouldn't be abnormal. This is
unusual only because our spiritual lives are so wretch-
edly sick and so far down from where they should be.

Can you Believe the Spirit is Lovable?

You must be satisfied, again, that there is nothing about
the Holy Spirit queer or strange or eerie. I believe it has
been the work of the devil to surround the person of the
Holy Spirit with an aura of queerness, or strangeness,
so that the people of God feel that this Spirit-filled life is
a life of being odd and peculiar, of being a bit uncanny.

That is not true, my friend! The devil manufactured
that. He hatched it out, the same devil that once said
to our ancient mother, "Yea, hath God said," and thus
maligned God Almighty. That same devil has maligned
the Holy Ghost. There is nothing eerie, nothing queer,
nothing contrary to the normal operations of the human
heart about the Holy Ghost. He is only the essence of
Jesus imparted to believers. You read the four Gospels
and see for yourself how wonderfully calm, pure, sane,
simple, sweet, natural and lovable Jesus was. Even phi-
losophers who don't believe in His deity have to admit

the lovableness of His character.

You must be sure of all this to the point of conviction. That is, you must be convinced to a point where you won't try to persuade God.

You don't have to persuade God at all. There is no persuasion necessary. Dr. A. B. Simpson used to say, "Being filled with the Spirit is as easy as breathing; you can simply breathe out and breathe in." He wrote a hymn to that effect. I am sorry that it is not a better hymn, because it is wonderful theology.

Can you Believe this is Scriptural?

Unless you have arrived at this place in your listening and thinking and meditating and praying, where you know that the Spirit-filled life is for you, that there is no doubt about it—no book you read or sermon you heard, or tract somebody sent you is bothering you; you are restful about all this; you are convinced that in the blood of Jesus when He died on the cross there was included, as a purchase of that blood, your right to a full, Spirit-filled life—unless you are convinced of that, unless you are convinced that it isn't an added, unusual, extra, deluxe something that you have to go to God and beg and beat your fists on the chair to get, I recommend this to you: I recommend that you don't do anything about it yet except to meditate upon the Scriptures bearing on this truth.

Go to the Word of God and to those parts of it which deal with the subject under discussion tonight and meditate upon them; for "faith cometh by hearing, and hearing by the word of God" (Romans 10:17). Real faith springs not out of sermons but out of the Word of God and out of sermons only so far as they are of the Word of God. I recommend that you be calm and confident about this. Don't get excited, don't despond. The darkest hour is just before the dawn. It may be that this moment of discouragement which you are going through is preliminary to a sunburst of new and beautiful living, if you will follow on to know the Lord.

Remember, fear is of the flesh and panic is of the

devil. Never fear and never get panicky. When they
came to Jesus nobody except a hypocrite ever needed
to fear Him. When a hypocrite came to Jesus He just
sliced him to bits and sent him away bleeding from ev-
ery pore. If they were ready to give up their sin and
follow the Lord and they came in simplicity of heart
and said, "Lord, what do You want me to do?" the Lord
took all the time in the world to talk to them and ex-
plain to them and to correct any false impressions or
wrong ideas they had. He is the sweetest, most under-
standing and wonderful Teacher in the world, and He
never panics anybody. It is sin that does that. If there is
a sense of panic upon your life, it may be because there
is sin in that life of yours which you need to get rid of.

Do you want to be Filled?

Again, before you can be filled with the Spirit you must
desire to be filled. Here I meet with a certain amount
of puzzlement. Somebody will say, "How is it that you
say to us that we must desire to be? Haven't we called
you on the phone? Aren't we out here tonight to hear
the sermon on the Holy Spirit? Isn't this all a comfort-
ing indication to you that we are desirous of being filled
with the Holy Spirit?"

Not necessarily, and I will explain why. For in-
stance, are you sure that you want to be possessed by
a spirit other than your own? Even though that spirit
be the pure Spirit of God? Even though He be the very
gentle essence of the gentle Jesus? Even though He be
sane and pure and free? Even though He be wisdom
personified, wisdom Himself, even though He have a
healing, precious ointment to distill? Even though He
be loving as the heart of God? That Spirit, if He ever
possess you, will be the Lord of your life!

Do you want Him to be Lord of your Life?

I ask you, Do you want Him to be Lord of you life? That
you want His benefits, I know. I take that for granted.
But do you want to be possessed by Him? Do you want

to hand the keys of your soul over to the Holy Spirit and say, "Lord, from now on I don't even have a key to my own house. I come and go as Thou tellest me"? Are you willing to give the office of your business establishment, your soul, over to the Lord and say to Jesus, "You sit in this chair and handle these telephones and boss the staff and be Lord of this outfit"? That is what I mean. Are you sure you want to do this? Are you sure that you desire it?

Are you sure that you want your personality to be taken over by One who will expect obedience to the written and living Word? Are you sure that you want your personality to be taken over by One who will not tolerate the self sins? For instance, self-love. You can no more have the Holy Ghost and have self-love than you can have purity and impurity at the same moment in the same place. He will not permit you to indulge self-confidence. Self-love, self-confidence, self-righteousness, self-admiration, self-aggrandizement and self-pity are under the interdiction of God Almighty, and He cannot send His mighty Spirit to possess the heart where these things are.

Again, I ask you if you desire to have your personality taken over by One who stands in sharp opposition to the world's easy ways. No tolerance of evil, no smiling at crooked jokes, no laughing off things that God hates. The Spirit of God, if He takes over, will bring you into opposition to the world just as Jesus was brought into opposition to it. The world crucified Jesus because they couldn't stand Him!

There was something in Him that rebuked them and they hated Him for it and finally crucified Him. The world hates the Holy Ghost as bad as they ever hated Jesus, the One from whom He proceeds. Are you sure, brother? You want His help, yes; you want a lot of His benefits, yes; but are you willing to go with Him in His opposition to the easygoing ways of the world? If you are not, you needn't apply for anything more than you have, because you don't want Him; you only think you do!

Are you sure you need Him?

Again, are you sure that you need to be filled? Can't you get along the way you are? You have been doing fairly well: You pray, you read your Bible, you give to missions, you enjoy singing hymns, you thank God you don't drink or gamble or attend movie theaters, that you are honest, that you have prayer at home. You are glad about all this. Can't you get along like that? Are you sure you need any more than that?

I want to be fair with you. I want to do what Jesus did: He turned around to them when they were following Him and told them the truth. I don't want to take you in under false pretense. "Are you sure you want to follow Me?" He asked, and a great many turned away. But Peter said, "Lord, to whom shall we go? thou hast the words of eternal life" (John 6:68). And the crowd that wouldn't turn away was the crowd that made history. The crowd that wouldn't turn back was the crowd that was there when the Holy Ghost came and filled all the place where they were sitting. The crowd that turned back never knew what it was all about.

But maybe you feel in your heart that you just can't go on as you are, that the level of spirituality to which you know yourself called is way beyond you. If you feel that there is something that you must have or your heart will never be satisfied, that there are levels of spirituality, mystic deeps and heights of spiritual communion, purity and power that you have never known, that there is fruit which you know you should bear and do not, victory which you know you should have and have not—I would say, "Come on," because God has something for you tonight.

There is a spiritual loneliness, an inner aloneness, an inner place where God brings the seeker, where he is as lonely as if there were not another member of the Church anywhere in the world. Ah, when you come there, there is a darkness of mind, an emptiness of heart, a loneliness of soul, but it is preliminary to the daybreak. O God, bring us, somehow, to the daybreak!

How to receive Him

Here is how to receive. First, present your body to Him (Romans 12:1–2). God can't fill what He can't have. Now I ask you: Are you ready to present your body with all of its functions and all that it contains—your mind, your personality, your spirit, your love, your ambitions, your all? That is the first thing. That is a simple, easy act—presenting your body. Are you willing to do it?

Now the second thing is to ask (Luke 11:9–13), and I set aside all theological objections to this text. They say that is not for today. Well, why did the Lord leave it in the Bible then? Why didn't He put it somewhere else? Why did He put it where I could see it if He didn't want me to believe it? It is all for us, and if the Lord wanted us to do it, He could give it without our asking, but He chooses to have us ask. "Ask of me, and I shall give thee" (Psalm 2:8) is always God's order; so why not ask?

Acts 5:32 tells us the third thing to do. God gives His Holy Spirit to them that obey Him. Are you ready to obey and do what you are asked to do? What would that be? Simply to live by the Scriptures as you understand them. Simple, but revolutionary.

The next thing is, have faith (Galatians 3:2). We receive Him by faith as we receive the Lord in salvation by faith. He comes as a gift of God to us in power. First He comes in some degree and measure when we are converted, otherwise we couldn't be converted. Without Him we couldn't be born again, because we are born of the Spirit. But I am talking about something different now, an advance over that. I am talking about His coming and possessing the full body and mind and life and heart, taking the whole personality over, gently, but directly and bluntly, and making it His, so that we may become a habitation of God through the Spirit.

So now suppose we sing. Let us sing "The Comforter Has Come," because He has come. If He hasn't come to your heart in fullness, He will; but He has come to earth. He is here and ready, when we present our vessel, to fill our vessel if we will ask and believe. Will you do it?

IV. HOW TO CULTIVATE THE SPIRIT'S COMPANIONSHIP

Can two walk together, except they be agreed?
Amos 3:3

Now this is what is known as a rhetorical question; it is equivalent to a positive declaration that two cannot walk together except they be agreed, and for two to walk together they must be in some sense one.

They also have to agree that they want to walk together, and they have to agree that it is to their advantage to travel together. I think you will see that it all adds up to this: for two to walk together voluntarily they must be, in some sense, one.

I am talking now about how we can cultivate the Spirit's fellowship, how we can walk with Him day by day and hour by hour—and you won't object if I say "you." (Sometimes we preachers preach in the third person, and you can develop a habit of thinking in the third person. We don't talk about "us"; we talk about "they." I don't like that. I think we ought to get personal about this.)

Are You Ready for this?

There are some of you who are not ready for this sermon at all. You are trying to face both ways at once. You are trying to take some of this world and to get some of that world over yonder. You are a Christian, but I am talking about an advance upon the first early stages of salvation and the cultivation of the presence of the Holy Ghost, so that He may illuminate and bless and lift and purify and direct your life. You are not ready for this, because you haven't given up all that you might have

the All. You want some, but you don't want all; that is
the reason you are not ready.

   You who have not given up the world will not be
able to understand what I am talking about. You want
Christianity for its insurance value. You want just what
a man wants when he takes out policy on his life, or his
car or his house. You don't want modernism, because
it hasn't any insurance value. You are willing to sup-
port this proposition financially. He would be a poor
man who would want insurance and not be willing to
pay for it. If Jesus Christ died for you on the cross you
are very happy about that because it means you won't
be brought into judgment, but have passed from death
into life. You are willing to live reasonably well, be-
cause that is the premium you are paying for the guar-
antee that God will bless you while you live and take
you home to heaven when you die!

   You may not be ready because your conception of
religion is social and not spiritual. There are people like
that. They have watered down the religion of the New
Testament until it has no strength in it. They have intro-
duced the water of their own opinion into it until it has
no taste left. They are socially minded. This is as far as
it goes with them. People like that they may be saved. I
am not prepared to say that they are not saved, but I am
prepared to say that they are not ready for what I am
talking about. The gospel of Christ is essentially spir-
itual, and Christian truth working upon human souls
by the Holy Ghost makes Christian men and women
spiritual.

   I don't want to say this, but I think that some of
you may not be ready for this message because you are
more influenced by the world than you are by the New
Testament. I am perfectly certain that I could rake up
fifteen boxcar loads of fundamentalist Christians this
hour in the city of Chicago who are more influenced in
their whole outlook by Hollywood than they are by the
Lord Jesus Christ. I am positive that much that passes
for the gospel in our day is very little more than a very
mild case of orthodox religion grafted on to a heart that

is sold out to the world in its pleasures and tastes and ambitions.

The kind of teaching that I have been giving has disturbed some people. I am not going to apologize at all, because, necessarily, if I have been traveling along thinking I am all right and there comes a man of God and tells me that there is yet much land to be possessed, it will disturb me. That is the preliminary twinge that comes to the soul that wants to know God. Whenever the Word of God hits us, it disturbs us. So don't be disturbed by the disturbance. Remember that it is quite normal. God has to jar us loose.

But there are some who are prepared. They are those who have made the grand, sweet committal. They have seen heaven draw nearer and earth recede; the things of this world have become less and less attractive, and the things of heaven have begun to pull and pull as the moon pulls at the sea, and they are prepared now. So I am going to give you these few little pointers to help you into a better life.

1. The Holy Spirit is a Living Person

The Holy Spirit is the third Person of the Trinity. He is Himself God, and as a Person, He can be cultivated; He can be wooed and cultivated the same as any person can be. People grow on us, and the Holy Spirit, being a Person, can grow on us.

2. Be Engrossed with Jesus Christ

Be engrossed with and honor Jesus Christ. John said: "But this spake he of the Spirit, which they that believe on him should receive: for the Holy Ghost was not yet given; because that Jesus was not yet glorified" (John 7:39).

I ask you to note that the Spirit was given when Jesus was glorified. Now that is a principle. Remember that He came and spread Himself out as a flood upon the people because Jesus was glorified. He established a principle, and He will never, never flood the life of any man except the man in whom Jesus is glorified.

Therefore, if you dedicate yourself to the glory of Jesus, the Holy Ghost will become the aggressor and will seek to know you and raise you and illumine you and fill you and bless you. Honoring Jesus Christ is doing the things which Jesus told you to do, trusting Him as your All, following Him as your Shepherd, and obeying Him fully.

Let's cultivate the Holy Ghost by honoring the Lord Jesus. As we honor Jesus, the Spirit of God becomes glad within us. He ceases to hold back, He relaxes and becomes intimate and communes and imparts Himself; and the sun comes up and heaven comes near as Jesus Christ becomes our all in all.

To glorify Jesus is the business of the Church, and to glorify Jesus is the work of the Holy Ghost. I can walk with Him when I am doing the same things He is doing, and go the same way He is going and travel at the same speed He is traveling. I must be engrossed with Jesus Christ. I must honor Him. "If any man serve me, him will my Father honour" (John 12:26). So let's honor the Lord Jesus. Not only theologically, but let's honor Him personally.

3. Walk in Righteousness

Let's walk in righteousness. The grace of God that bringeth salvation also teaches the heart that we should deny ungodliness and worldly lusts and live soberly and righteously and godly in this present world. There you have the three dimensions of life. Soberly—that is me. Righteously—that is my fellowman. Godly—that is God. Let us not make the mistake of thinking we can be spiritual and not be good. Let's not make the mistake of thinking we can walk with the Holy Ghost and go a wrong or dirty or an unrighteous way, for how can two walk together except they be agreed? He is the Holy Spirit, and if I walk in an unholy way, how can I fellowship with Him?

4. Make your Thoughts a Clean Sanctuary

To God, our thoughts are things. Our thoughts are the decorations inside the sanctuary where we live. If our thoughts are purified by the blood of Christ, we are living in a clean room no matter if we are wearing overalls covered with grease. Your thoughts pretty much decide the mood and weather and climate inside your heart, and God considers your thoughts as part of you.

Thoughts of peace, thoughts of pity, thoughts of charity, thoughts of God, thoughts of the Son of God— these are pure things, good things and high things. Therefore, if you would cultivate the Spirit's acquaintance, you must get hold of your thoughts and not allow your mind to be a wilderness in which every kind of unclean beast roams and bird flies. You must have a clean heart.

5. Seek to Know Him in the Word

It is in the Word we find the Holy Spirit. Don't read too many other things. Some of you will say, "Look who's talking!" Well, go ahead and say it, I don't mind; but I am reading fewer and fewer things as I get older, not because I am losing interest in this great big old suffering world, but because I am gaining interest in that other world above. So I say, don't try to know everything. You can't. Find Him in the Word, for the Holy Ghost wrote this Book. He inspired it, and He will be revealed in its pages.

What is the word when we come to the Bible? It is meditate. We are to come to the Bible and meditate. That is what the old saints did. They meditated. They laid the Bible on their old-fashioned handmade chair, got down on the old, scrubbed board floor and meditated on the Word. As they meditated, faith mounted. The Spirit and faith illuminated. They had nothing but a Bible with fine print and narrow margins and poor paper, but they knew their Bible better than some of us with all our helps. Let's practice the art of Bible meditation.

Now please don't grab that phrase book and go out and form a club. Don't do it! Just meditate. That is what we need. We are organized to death already. Let's just be plain Christians. Let's open the Bible, spread it out on the chair, and meditate on it. It will open itself to us, and the Spirit of God will come and brood over it.

So be a meditator. I challenge you, try it for a month and see how it works. Put away questions and answers and the filling in of blank lines about Noah. Put all that cheap trash away and take a Bible, open it, get on your knees and say, "Father, here I am. Begin to teach me." He will begin to teach you, and He will teach you about Himself and about Jesus and about God and about the Word and about life and death and heaven and hell, and about His own presence.

6. Cultivate the Art of Recognizing the Presence of the Spirit

I have just one more point: Cultivate the art of recognizing the presence of the Spirit everywhere. Get acquainted with the Holy Ghost and then begin to cultivate His presence. When you wake in the morning, in place of burying your head behind the Tribune, couldn't you get in just a few thoughts of God while you eat your grapefruit?

Remember, cultivating the Holy Ghost's acquaintance is a job. It is something you do, and yet it is so easy and delightful. It is like cultivating your baby's acquaintance. You know when you first look at the little wrinkled fellow, yelling, all mouth, you don't know him. He is a little stranger to you. Then you begin to cultivate him, and he smiles. (It isn't a smile at all. He has colic! You think it is a smile, and it is such a delight.) Pretty soon he wiggles an arm, and you think he is waving at you. Then he gurgles and you think he said "mama." You get acquainted!

Is this for ministers? Is it for housewives? Yes— housewives and clerks and milkmen and students. If you will thus see it and thus believe it and thus surrender to it, there won't be a secular store in the pavement. There won't be a common, profane deed that you will ever do. The most menial task can become a priestly ministration when the Holy Ghost takes over and Christ becomes your all in all.

CPSIA information can be obtained
at www.ICGtesting.com
Printed in the USA
LVOW12s2005021217
558425LV00001B/98/P

GHOST

SENTENCE

POEMS

MARY

FLANAGAN

atmosphere press

TABLE OF CONTENTS

"Of all ghosts the ghosts of our old loves
are the worst."

~ Arthur Conan Doyle

The heart is stronger than the bullet, until

A VESSEL

You tell me you're from
Behind the iron curtain
Yet we both know
That ship's a little rusty
Holes stuffed
With gum wrappers and selfies
Caved in from online shopping
Heavy undulation
Waves, shining pills pop to the
Surface
It turns out iron isn't forever
Just strong
Enough to
Weather the men crying
For a while, great submerged fleets
Lying dead like whale bodies. So what do we
Have now, washed up
On flooded riverbanks   new
Borders scratched red on our skin
Our machine-parsed
Words will never oxidize
        so therefore
        some machine or other
Knows that I love
The lost scent of ocean
In your hair

ELECTION

The lady in the video
Turns both hands and wrenches
Them like she's killing a chicken
She's sitting in front
Of a cheap copied
Landscape painting
Her hands enact a moment
Not as picturesque
As the story of Mount Monadnock
How 400 million years ago
Wolves dug and dug
Kicking back dirt to make a hill so high
Even Emerson would call it a Titan; yet
Heavens—he did have his
High hopes smashed
Finding but a beggar

Wading through the trails   Men of
Bone, lashed to an
Old gas lamppost   unreasoned
The river no longer needs a
Guardian

They say it's a kind of abuse
That sticks with you like a thorn
In the paw

EMAIL

you know this goes to space
every time I click send...
then it goes to spam

there are infinite parallel universes
in one of them I spam you every day
in another we go see shows

today our notes avoided us
for 7 hours. this is proof
where could they have gone?

basking on the greek isle syros
nibbling fresh caught fish
from a pure white balcony

are there fish left in greece?
do tomatoes still ripen in
the light of car bombs?

it's hard not to
interpret meaning
from absence

jupiter tumbles close in the night sky
einstein's cousin looks south and thinks:
never trust a planet even if it's been dead forty years

last night my laptop sent you mail
and wove all kinds of
fictions into your absence

TANGLED

On a scale of one to ten, how
Intoxicated would you say
You are?
It is not what you don't do
It's just that you admitted
Something over nothing. For
There never was no man nowhere so virtuous
So it would not be unreasonable
Not to have a pre-emptive strike
I couldn't not help it
By which I actually mean an unprovoked attack
Not to conclude that it is reasonably likely
That a rights violation is about to occur. After all,
Do you believe that contrary to what the media says,
Raising taxes does not create jobs?

TRUTH

You will never be ignored again
Said the new fascist

Never beaten again
Extolled Slobodan Milošević
(In similar vocal pitch)

Truth, an old toothless lion
In the hands of a skilled ringmaster

Who has some corporate tie-in
To golf resorts and casinos but
Embarrassment won't stick to

Plastic grass in Paris
Without shame to

Block a nefarious prince
If one owns whole dimensions
Untouchable   virtual

Messages, thirty
Years apart ring identical

Resentments, tentacled
Years of war crimes
Boundless

The wall is brown, you say
But I see the hue and it is

As bright as horizon

A wall most certainly blue
Caribbean ocean view

Assuredly you say I need my
Eyes checked, I must be colorblind

That is how it works, you see
You claim to know a rightness
Against supporting evidence

O! if our conned heroes could
Eagle themselves, snap into bulldozers

It takes time to convince
Those with riding mowers
To tumble the capitol

And bury for once
This sullied map

INSUBSTANTIAL STUFF
OF PURE BEING

Unbeknownst to me, a door opens under our bed. For a moment there is transference, as though bound trains puff the sky. I know from the drip marks all about men's viscosity. Just think, we might have been clarinets with all that wandering. Black instruments. No one has properly named desire, except by what is untasted, even festering. There—with this giant girl, no acts of dominion. A smokehouse, this city, making lost sponges indivisible to touch. The sky holds unsleeping, tired-out angels. A terrible insult is this skirt, clotted in gold.

YOU, WITCH

I Gretel myself through your thickets and stands
The water is rising, our own cursed history
Something baked and fresh pouring
From the drowning windows this steam
Creates you
I'm not one to stuff myself with crepes, cupcakes but
There, you offer me chocolate and gin
Sweet smoke from your witch-mouth

I take
    and take succumbing sugar

 Succor sustenance

Like the captain who knows his inevitable
Dark and stormy fate, I swim with purpose
I man your uncertainty
I man your declarations
Of a feminine soul, I brave
My back against the seaswept forest dunking
Around our boat these whole trunks punch
And suck into an eternal rhythm

Water's own breathing
Out-In the path huffs before me

Covered in drippy sweetness, filled with logs

Your spell crafts a cornered intimacy
That waits for anyone on this path
Pouncer
You open wide the peacock blue doors of your

La Canache
Anyone curious enough for fresh bread
Anyone with a finger reaching toward the honey
Gathered by

Lavender mouths

   At my desk
I don't daydream of sugar. I am not

Addicted to cookies   I don't bend to
Advertising   how to fill my mouth
What is sweetness. We are on a whale now, the forest
But a tiny fur, then you cross. You crease.
You flood my mouth with sweetness
You lay a certain path for hungry children to find your
Word house. Hot house.
Take advantage house.

Steaming with (woodsmoke) (flames)
(Path to Treasure Island) (Stephenson)
(Ahoy) (Land Ho) (Full sail ahead)

You whose witch-words conjure
Shapely sirens, safe-bets, we march into
Revolution
Cauldrons, cupcakes
Weapons stuffed with
Wintermelon
Raspberry filling smears the bullets
In my fist

LOVE AND GUNS

Yes I see the strangeness of it
How we thrive amongst hard pressed
Metal how I write to you the longest
Letters in elegant penmanship
As though ink jots from my teeth
Each gun eats
Metal meat for
                    jaundice
Is it because every
Blood-filled body
Hides a bucket of hate
In the lungs
So breathing naturally
Labors under the pressure that
Pushes like magnets against
The puned the pruned pure love

HOW TO READ A GHOST SENTENCE

Since foxes believe that the world furs around them, they think they can feed reality. No one should use words for questions. Even though foxes know that what they're writing or saying is barking the truth.

We are nocturnal. Ghosts fill our lungs and hold our hands at night. Giggles fill our lutes and hold our handguns at streetlight. To see an apparition you need to look up. Lead your giraffe by stalking the stars. Read a ghost sentence by watching the sky.

TRUTH PROCEDURES

rates should be low
should
measure

my
beating
bones

thin
and snappable
percentages

(wishing)

bones
stronger than

conjunctions
then, after wanton gristle
subtracts

(is salt)

a promise to
find my name:

names of shoes or clothes
food or music
once

there
were songs
that starved for names

woven
buoyant
names

names that
puppet
the reach of fingers

names that
used to be
music

WHAT PEOPLE DO ON SUNDAYS

sleep too much in avoidance
of what makes the earth brown

think of visiting someone
one forgot is now dead

watch for snow   the grass   is
greening and it shouldn't

wait to see if something moves
anything

THE NIGHT I MET A VAMPIRE

You stain my bones
The shade of your young old
Eyes   Your name buried
Beneath my lavender
A sliver of brown
Paper listens and shifts
Makes a small gaping tunnel to
Open
To call you   You

Emailed me last
Night while I slept to
Tell me you were
On a bus. It was 6am
The sky dripped with
Madeira My
Tongue turns black
With the sweetness
Pouring from your
Voice You flood
My hair while
I sleep. I sleep

And you watch
A face I never
Quite recall across the
Twenty masks you
Were granted at
Twenty massacres
The photo of a child
Sits on a small window-dresser
A paperback listens and shifts

Bright bright birth these
Are all you   You
In your angles and
Elsewheres
My cheek forges your
Breastbone, drifting and listing
Above long armadas, your
Treasure chest

We lift-off openness
The moon waits and watches
She knows no better than
Ghosting   You
Here before me
You
Who know nothing other than
The fog of my bones

Your lightness
The spin of the earth
Presses us, two imperfect
Flowers in a book

THE GODS OF THE NORTH EXHALE

the sky summons the ghost of your grayness
a felt-furred light leaks from your

wrists   steaming each window
we pass, the glass and your eyes
hold the same pale glow

stone light flesh light fashed
this is so and real and true

as is permanence in impermanence
the icy box of forgetting you hide
deep down in smoke filled pockets

the sky hides in the shadows
stealing more of your north sea

mourning as though
the tops of buildings
the very sun   these antler

your incense   your ink-dripped voice
their very own breath

MINISTERING A FLOOD
(UPDATE WITH GOD I)

Holy Savior, or some such
divine wind, make
these simple pleas
your own life's mission:
Holy Savior, stain my
glasses with your solutions
(pictures, please). The kids left all
of their chores, rapunzelled out windows,
stuffed themselves into animals
and have gotten out whole
through the hold. Just so you know,
we noticed that at least the mammals
can talk. Holy Savior, please
make animals again
from all the girls'
heeled boots

WOODCUTTER

Some being or influence contains
your glass bottle—pilfering

oxygen from sleeping leaves
who startle awake, dread to

plummet; you whose wandering
fingers trace birch skin

to read quiet today's news
You have brailled from my tongue

lost instructions.
Nightman, your trumpet legs

what in me meets you
there, knows the door's blush?

You face away from the sea to
measure the land. From fire

your eyes chop wood, build
houses, give them away. Hide

the taxes. Such a turbid
wind carves your face

all current and colors. Nothing
the sea says beckons

more axes, more unbelievable
flannel, tromp boots

You stash mighty oxen
in your lunch box. Men

give you plank
dinner parties

bravely, all night
you walk them

YOUR BEDROOM

I pay a Russian woman
To put me on a rack
And make demands
As if caught in a fever
Her name is Milla
          Tuck your J-Bits
Somehow the year has made
Voltage onto us
I remember you hung a fox
From your chamber
With thin brown twine
          Blood wasn't built in a day
And her—
The heaving booms
Under her keep
Such is joy: clarity,
Christmas   Your strikes make
My face hurt
          Ridiculous oppositions
The map you wear flies
In the face of certain logics
Your strokes take on
The orchestras
          Suck that stick up your Yu Yu
I can live in such forests
I thrive with such pleas
Trailing the groping fool
Breadcrumbs
Along the grass floor
          Zip it!
A code for California

Brittle bones
Where do you hang your fox
When it must
Sleep

THE EVENT AND THE SUBJECT

1.

      Take away
something hot and
memorable. Take my life or
my sunglasses. With
dishrag in hand, you
declare your animosities
as if I am fast-changing
cloud-conjuring rain.
As if I am miles away storm.

If only I could show you
bristles of things and
their misgivings.
Your mouth remains
voracious. You have
masticated war and earth
to save your maps. Your
gone-mother places rough
palms, her halo deficient
at such proximity to stop the
world leader.

2.

        You are
tundral. Brief episode
walking. Your roar herds
insects and toothbrushes. This
habit leaves city bathrooms in
a tidy state. Before 4pm, no one
holds hands or feeds each other
cake. This is the only fallow of
tree time: Trees floom out of season
to assault the coldness we become.
Trees bear arms—

We collect
plastic coins. I hold
in my arms small babies
and their mathering cries until
the batteries run out. Without
batteries they all stop eating
and drinking. No sewing of clothes.

3.

      In my room the tough
curl of sun slowly marks unfurling
territory. So many ways to
cooperate with the trombone,
applaud, unfold delicate
paper with gritty fingernails. There
lies such joy in this box, the
irreplaceable. Birches send missives—
walking sticks and inch worms. No
insects are ascribed to letters,
only measurements. There are
too many now, undulating the branches
filling the clouds.

Jeans fall, impersonate
caterpillar wings. Change is here.
Hands tip arm for honeywine
that sticks to the envelopes
strung around the bed.
We sleep among letters. Oaks
counter, pin our arks,
dogs drip the backseat and
dream of defenestration
watching dashed
lines solidify.

4.

      You are
viscous and honeycombed
trying to make a girl
out of dirty water. A set of
objects inscribed with a
professional's obscure rules.
We have never made love
in the kitchen and I want
to know if you are bread
or butter or syrup.

HIBOU

Horsefly
Every night a great
Horned grandfather calls
Over a westward LA streetwalker
The trees too dense there seep
Many poisons in the mouse bodies
Pokies in the mouth-bogs
The feathered sentinel
Returns   but there you are again

Hope
In a nightdress   I horsewoman soup without a
Transplant I hope each sound is not
Transaction   I want there to be a
Universal consistent truth in you   Nations turn
Back, suspicious   blackening
I want urchins and dinners
Where is our touching
The witness   is there no optimism left in you?

Horizon
A shrinking girl, a glacier
Grinds by in her angry
Range Rover, bared teeth
Transform the delicate
Skunk of her skin, her face biting
The ashed air in her
Smiled failings
Rise   dripping   I put one

Hell
Is what other people and I

Have all made   a monument
I put one ear to the
Sky listening for calls
The other to the damp earth   where
Burrowed Cicadas wait
Thirteen years
Hoping for heartbeats

POET

Caught forever
In a blurred pillow
Can I transubstantiate?
My nerve after all suggests
Such timbers
My name suggests
Such throes, virginal passion
I can't stop
The asking   wanting
Stop my suffering
Tell me, from the tops of bricks
About the government
Its mealy fictions
There are lines crossed
Tell me, from the tracks of buildings
About the gravel
There are lobbies that
Have blended
You know I can see it too
Your smoke
A material with a thirst
A mathematics
Of your self-story
Forests the farm
Of certain
Gospels
Why did you come so hungry
Keep a girl, for once
Keep me goddess, for a time

MINISTERING A TORNADO
(UPDATE WITH GOD II)

This morning, leaves still cling to the trees, but
the sun is telling them to drop dead. The heavens fill
with saws, dust, fill with cuts of fabric in
brown and yellow patterns, with baskets and dogs and
men who need tribulation. So much filing through
this place, oxen roads heaving left, then right. Thank
you for the nuns
          and trips to the symphony. The
drama of it: experience a body washed entirely
in kidney sounds. There is an instance of Paul Bunyan
in my house, but it is not the same as yesterday. He
tells the leaves up there to go for it, blands potatoes,
builds benches to dangle the feet, gets on with cuts
          and bruises,
consecrates with sweat the inadequacies of paper
towels and flannel

[the spell lingering from breakfast, your mouth

voracious as always]

BEING TRANSFORMED
INTO A PHOENIX

You had better not fucking die
because I need you to kill me first
yes—plan it, bury the body
when it comes to that, but
not today

I get to die first, amidst small murmurs
a tiny creaking door to elsewhere a child's lips open just
so, rapt with hero's tales   carry me oh jousting steed
oh shaman's magic smoke oh coffee oh breakfasts
tomorrow

is not here, not yet anyway, I don't want
to pour out the wine—blanket me
away fold me into you, you who are comfortable and
worn and fearless I get to die first, hear me!
only yesterday

I turned a cha cha cha in the catacombs
pressed close the swarthy roots of trees; they dipped
me so low my hair kissed rotting logs   draped along
empty noses   the music slowed
today

know my little request, with the sweet end of time
held in my mouth   the heartbeat
slows under the skin of the
world   cut and changed
forever

PARKING LOT AT WHOLE FOODS

She's slumped in the banged up
Black Lexus as I run

Through the shiny black lot in rain
Dark corner painted darker

A window shade perched
To hide the needle in her calf

From the moon
Her woven shirt hung to

Block the other windows
She will awake

Before dawn, a wolf with light
In her eyes

She will awake

AS IF SEEMINGLY SEALED SHUT

Everyone knows it's not safe to
Go out on a brimstone night
Especially with you

       I admit   I'm fidgety
Restless legislators leisures
How long will you highroad this headiness
Rootless   legs
       lemmings
I darken your scent to a secret cliff

   Teetering, you declare
you do not feel correct
         precise   actual
               What is
correct to we bodied beasts?

And it is home to the pagan heather
bees
    harrowing
  honeying   quick now—quick
before anyone sees
There is no need to carve
Our ranges and huffing

I know blossoms forest your chest

the sun inhales
Skyline   gulls wishbone words

That blouse our very skin

there lies a *here* within us
lighthouse

the depths of your thick sea
A fragrance does not lie

TWO MAGICIANS

Follow Me / Flow shepherded / Furrow the bleating /
my
  breath borrowing

      Who will be my light leman? Layman—

You threw me / Lay me /
Tossed aside all pride

Lie and ravage. Lemoning. Wring and wrought /
Willful. Two
enchanters / their fast-life spells
   this is my strength.

The string. I string you. Sing you / Hymn

O mighty course of stars / I bird and collect / You are
my breath feather /
curled and quivered

Row and rustle. Rise. Golden Doves.
Dove. Dove.
  Done for.

Something about you gills / puffs and glistens /
listens /
The speckled scales shift
  polka dot drift

        Bolted fury

Springs the door   Tongues the rusted
trellis

Quiet. Quench. Red cheeks champ
delicate fangs
  delicious sorcery /

        When yon hill ears twitch. Hilly nose flinch.

Rabbit your strength and arrows / lie open to me.
Let blanket / blanketed

O comforter, O agitator
Let linger these cool hands /

DEAR SIR, A CONFESSION

I rant and bend
For there is wild in me
I tear and lip
For wildness eagers me
With a hunger
Never food
Where be souled experience?
Even when I read
A wild pushes me
Connect and remember she says
Arousing thunder
This is feral
This is not of now
This you will likely never understand
For I do not
All my untamed mindfulness
In all my primitive howling at the stars
Water-slip truths into ocean
I gnaw
A hot core of knowing
I bite raw

FEVER

Vibrating down streets divinity has
Somehow kissed
Word particles swarm
Around us
You, soaked in
What's behind me, the night sky
Brings such a fever
Do I mistake your heat for
High resonance
Two bees hone in on the same yellow daisy
Disagreeing about whose
Prickled legs will carry away
Dusty, heaving golden futures

THE QUESTION OF THE ONE

declaring nothing at all
the randomist gathers rebellious charts
documents specific weaknesses, months

of our unknowing   Apples lift
one side of her makeshift ledger
to a turbid dance   So we vote

while she predicts ethereal profit
an aware-stitched hem
shapes a dress to cover

[shame and loss]

two figures hint at her body
the mouth myth
the nest territory   ravens steal away

complete empty sets
the randomist comprehends
shadow-figures on the bridge

ready to jump   neither he nor she
neither painter or painted
tinted to insult the sky

[in the agreement]

scented umbrance of graphite
on the skin, they are pushed there by
tabulations   multiplied into an embrace

heaven knows, it is
a new day, pooling
these our faces

back at us,
to ask
is it now?

MATTERING

God can see

A dash rot on a black soul on a black nightmare

But the figure lives in a large white house

Pale skin billowing, palms palpitating

Around the cars in the parking lot

Skin color here is tied to cruelty   crusade

Brothers scream from bruises and cry for justice

The gods and devils must hear our cudgels

You laugh in the devil's face

Law in the blond devil's factor

Nonetheless he or she

Vocabularies, visits, and stays

Like a friend whose job lost a shit job

And didn't have plan b

But in this case

The devil needs no diagnosis

I WISH FOR A VERSION OF YOU
TO SAVE ME

There is another
Suitor you know   he has
Put me in a tower
Built right onto the
Top of his car   he drives
Me around   my hair tumbles

Out the highest window
Trapped inside cold stone:
Me, supposed to perform
Alchemy or talk to very
Small men who want me to
Do even more stuff for them
Than you: Goldspinning

Giving birth   listen—
In the forest this
Tower-car is quite a sight
And yes, the windows steam up
Making it rain inside yet
My lips are left without
All the precious

Tiny-types of kindness
—Touch my face
Give me warmness
Along with hotness
A girl can take
Only so much heavy
Breathing

MINISTERING THE BATTLE BETWEEN GOOD AND EVIL (UPDATE WITH GOD III)

I carry *top already* water, above

the dark grey shale

the soldier is half way in the ground

determining   place as

embrasure

some-share

a doorway   a *somewhere*

the soldier draws deadlines

moves in both worlds

since the tear

of extreme confidence:

bullets are transfixed

red by the baseball

the stags

garbage-bear signs on a

   cross-filled country, they advertise "freedom"

(you seek to stuff devils into a sack—

and you do it!)

the truck trundles this with the men in back:
looking for their sister's face oh! saint-inclined savior
we who follow the nonsense of seeds
saving harvests of various shapes and stricture

the women bunt with *négligemment*
their   ruffled handkerchiefs
stifle the sun as they work

(the body cultivates displacement
grows damper, plates shift)

your rockmaking sounds
quickly –
                I will pay attention to the length
of your righteous weapons
your *wonderwater*
just now, the feverish wire of the soldier reaches

a wife with no name
    who does not make it into
 the episodes

(another diablo, another bag—

you fill it!)

I shall give attention to

the length of your god-arms stuffing garbage

underwater

      the danger under the ocean below

the pontoon above

always starting over   under

the darkness

[the *Law of Original Horizontality* states that most sediments, when originally formed, were laid down horizontally]

A PURE SUBJECTIVE COMMITMENT IS POSSIBLE

I'll tell you what it is. I'll hand you outcry.
We drive. Grey commandeers the car and exhausts
your mouth. Notions of truth-telling. Road bends—
   we see over brushwood thickets.

Dressed for Sunday, mopmakers
whose hands have scrubbed
corners from church toilets, stillborn pennies; easy—
   find a course of violet, tie a small cloth.

Instructions for living in coal mines. We peat a little,
sinking. After confessions and ammonia. After
coughing, caring for the small too cold ones. Here—
   mothers bring final things.

Little knots on trees make a sorry each
mighty woods bend heavy, hair locks bear tiny socks,
keen those hands. How
   we come to blessing.

INTRODUCTION TO BEING AND EVENT

the obliging sky
slides down
into cocktail
parties
into orange-
sweatered
idealist men

who later *tumble*
from stars and
trap doors

above
this tableau,
horses
bloat quickly
rivers swell
over the
sill

the trajectorian
his aim
his *order*

clutches
banana-weapon
bears bright
headphones
mutters of
his
hunger

WHICH ISSUES

Demons and scurvy
will relentlessly attack us

the men say

Lie about us   divide
the rats
  these next four years

We are asked the following questions.

Which issue(s) ultimately influence your decisions?
Select as many as apply
o   Illegal immigrationing
o   Radical Islamic terrorismos
o   The Supremecy Court
o   Economy/jobs/outscourcing
o   Barter honchos
o   Scarcity of life
o   Obama Playing Cards
o   Religious Libel
o   Veteran Culinary Habits
o   Taxation without Representation
o   Debit Cards
o   Other

Note that 75% of each contribution will be designated
not towards these issues but toward either the 2020
primary (which shall be the default) or 2020 election
fund. Party!

FASCIST LOVE SONG

I PLIGHT

ALLIGATORS

TO THE

FLAME-THROWER

OF THE

UNITED

FASCHETTES

OF UNMAGICA

AND TO THE

REPULSION FOR

WHICH IT STANDS

ONE NAVEL

GOING UNDER

WITHOUT RESCUE

WITH COVFEFE

AND JUSTIFICATIONS

U-HAUL

THE ONLY RESPITE

      Vermont Raw
Meyer Lemon
Orange Blossoms gave their throats
Plastic Bear-Clear Clover
Waxy Rosemary
Lavandre des virtues

      Collectors
Small quaking wonders
Drop to the ground a
Layer so thick the Dead
Can be scraped together
By the double handful

      Across my threshold
You neatly place pots and
Jars into which
My fingers
Glide vampire
Mouthfuls

AN EMBRACE OF SINGULARITIES

I declare you. I cast you in untenable body positions. I see your words float away garter-blue. If you were to ride a truth, the roof would rise up to the clouds. Everyone is leaning and changed right. An oboe says, "I can't say a single thing to you." Faces turn away. Await Humming.

You have rerouted my train. You are wearing vibrant sky-dyed tennies and think you know. You reek of ketchup and fries. You hold electronics diagrams and think you understand my body. Save your looking, your cream at midnight, white in light under these fifteen-foot ceilings. Save your shares and your tight-jeaned-ass—you, who only know how to judge.

Not Right. Not Right. The train is wailing, a baby is missing her pink shoe, gum sticking the foot to a thousand concretes. People stare into their shining palms. Burn stakes its claim in teeth, sucking men from dark du-rags. The men are not crying for help, but you pity them anyway. You do nothing. People are taken from restaurants in the dead of night. This you smells of grease and soft, undercooked bread. Sing into your umbrella. The ground shakes, drunk men unfold from the concrete, springing upright, wearing striped shirts. They all have accents and appear fresh, young, and optimistic. They think they know.

Just like you. The city is courting bites, asks me to polish silver, making sounds fit for no one's ears. In the city, we may diagram the contest: you read it, keep a nest filled with city-blue eggs. You dug a trench not knowing. Rabbits lose a foot there. Sparrows see air, not glass, and crash. We saw one fall. And when rabbits drawl their red paint onto your snow, when feathers find their holy father in your stare, you cannot say you know. Promise me.

Right now I am also a homeless. Right now I sit on orange and yellow. As soon as my tags trunk to possibility. As soon as voices give someone quiet. As soon as these young men take off their hats and permit the head to be transcribed in image recognition.

As soon as my hair will hold hot pink. As soon as young girls pull their hair up and detach the fur from the years. As soon as the supermodel decides on her volunteer army. As soon as soup kitchens really make soup.

As soon as lawyers, universities, and plastic surgeons stop advertising want. As soon as my 10,000 steps are pain-free. As soon as ink reconfigures underneath my skin. The city shoots screeches fit for no one's ears. As soon as men stop their spraying. As soon as god takes a stand, and tells Quakers to never attempt gospel tunes. If it were so easy to find a Sunday. If it were so easy to jack up your shorts and get fucked for money. If you had no idea someone was stacking your hair and blue Zinnias in a locked box for when you die.

I take account of a jaundiced man and his underground arguments. I hold the women with puffy tennies, frustrated with me and with cleaning. Our hands ache. I hold. I hold. Men in blue shoes and jumpsuits saunter in, sending out a few monochromatic whistles.

ENOUGH

You know what I want to have with you?

A You Can Do No Wrong
Love

It might not be the same as

We've Weathered Many Storms
Love

Or
I'm Sick Can You Share My Pain
Love

Or
Why Did You Cheat On Me
Love

Or
We Lost The Baby
Love

Rather can we tune our radios
To another unconditional
Universe

Without carving into the slippery sea
Without touching the

Earth at all

EQUINOX

Greedy for more seconds to rub my
Tufted chin along your saddled shoulders
You laugh at me, saying   Time

It's in my head
For our hoofbeats and breaths mark us
Forever present   We

Shudder to a stop on Jane Street
Snort impatiently at the fire in
The sky over Hoboken   Finally we

Reach our necks to the blue souled
Ripples of the river   To wish

INEVITABLE

You: a beautiful cracked tub
In a creaky old manse

Running so hot you
Scald then

Turn to ice, snapping
Off my fingers

But it may be your feet I admire most
They show you are half

Lion
Your delicate lip

Is no match
For the hidden

Balance somewhere
Deep inside, when you perch

I plug you, mix your halves
For a time, make peace with

City and tundra, the long grasses of a feral summer
The rising steam of the hot springs that sketch

Words and shapes across
Our winter's window

MS. TOO-MANY-WORDS

So I know I emailed
Too many variations of
My thoughts to you. It wasn't
The best idea.

So I can understand why you
Might think "wow, she's
Something else." And maybe
Not in a good something-else way.

What if I told you I hosted
You in my dreams, one of many debates
On Kantian knowledge in a Brooklyn diner?
These are necessary truths

For your curious gestures
Confuse me, and I like
The way you speak in leaps, in omelets,
In steam from coffee so thick

I can't see your face   only shapes
Made by bright little
Halos when I close
My heavy fluorescent eyes

YOU MAY BE MY MUSE
BUT YOU MAKE A SHITTY BOYFRIEND

Plates collide and the earth shifts
Eating shipyards on its backbone
You boffin around my doorstep
One of the five million toothbrushes of debris
In the sea, you are old hollow wood
Repeating strangers from your last book
Yet for so long I longed, I stretched
I pulled into you thinking
        this is someone who feels
Hundreds of thousands of volts
Moved between us in
Six moonlights   but still
There lies no skirmish to
Sister my teeth into, nothing solid
To grab as the water rivers us—
You earthquake my ocean floor
My ode flower with a glance, centuries
Of *built* string between our matched
Tectonics made more distant
With the slippery clay of
Language, words that never
Really meet, never sit down and say
Thank you or *Are you near* or
Can you swim? So I leave you, I do not
Follow the autobiography of your tongue
And the earth drowses miles under
The grimy sea as I write this

TODAY I FINISH GHOST SENTENCE WITH 'LEAVING'

I have trouble staying and going, trouble making decisions since things went south. Maybe in the woods. I should go high in the woods. I should go north to the woods. Woods are good in the summer and lonely in winter. Islands. Bugs are always busy and I will be too. I should forage. Hide from the cameras. Just when I tried to call home. Home is somewhere I must leave.

This is the right property for you, she said. The right property. How can she possibly know? How can she possibly know? Who knows what the right house is? Who knows what the right job is? Or the most perfect shoes? Which choices avoid plastics, silver halide, mercury? Which is the better love? Whose country loves more art? What language has 31 words for snow?

Which brand of toothpaste from the hundreds of brands of toothpaste lined up on the pharmacy shelves? Which One? Which One?

Mean.

You were mean. Mean and taught me to not know. Mean and conniving America, endless toothpaste for pickety smiles. Endless dental bounty. Endless promises and paper towels. Endless end tables and frozen dinners. Endless toilet paper. Too much choice America. Too much time spent choosing.

How to tell what road America, the righteous path? How could she possibly know the right land? How could she possibly know the right town? Did she walk the magic ricepaper for deeper insight America? The pale belly of the powerplant splits open to spew brown blood. Kimosabe what have you done with my horse? Where is my mask, my gun?

My confusion is mundane. My confusion is mundane. She thinks I am an artist and I am merely mundane. I need to pretend. Pretend that no one thinks about the brand of toilet paper. Pretend that toilets do not defecate Miami and Venice. Play deaf. Each phone to shining phone. Drone to drone. From each drone the brand of toilet paper lurks immanent. Men advise women. Women call their mothers. From the shelves to shining shelves of toilet America, trees surrender their rings America, my father hocked his wedding ring for toilet paper and an alarm clock. After the war. After the war. After the pool has dried, make another. Here we are. Another war. This time, inside.

Our toilet speaks priorities. Birds cough out their lungs, fly with regret to places where their feet no longer freeze in ice. Birds start falling. Bees lie dying. Men make people into blood across the sea, bringing the bottles home with them.

Newspapers, how can you possibly know what to print, how can anything precede anything? When you are accused of untruth then who owns actuality? How can you, pair of shoes, justify your going on sale? Who exactly is making shoes and typing and answering phones?

Phoenixing from the excess I look down. From the spectacle I look down. All of my waste. Our cellophane. When confronted I look down. I look down. I look down and see how friendly concrete is. How friendly concrete likes to grow and cover. Hold me concrete, your arms are warm and breathe summer. I look down and watch a falling baby hit its head and thunk.

It is crowded and I do not know which road. Did she say left? Whose shame is this? I am lonely and I do not know which toothpaste. We are either watchers getting fat or doers starving and dying. We are alone. I look down. Baby how can you give me your secret book of lizards? Keep them close. Keep your fingers. Fingers in mouth and point. Pointing at something makes it real. Weigh anchor, baby, here comes the water.

And there is blood staining the street. Blood staining the teeth. Feet push platforms to be above water. Skin stretches, marked from pain to be real. Pain in the low hum of refrigerators I can hear crying softly in every kitchen in this city. When refrigerators cry, lights hum a monk drone of pity. Lights have pity and refrigerators lie. The baby closes its book and cries. Toothpaste falls to the concrete and cries. I look down. How the people are sighing. How they wail in raided restaurants in the night and sent away. Whose shame.

Don't tell me you aren't listening. The city is leaving. The big one is leaving. A man in a ratty gorilla suit exits his 10th Street apartment. My stacks of postmodernist criticism are post-leaving. No one knows where they will shelter. My laundry is leaving, dark shrubs shuffling down the stairs. You're leaving me in the pools of blood the men brought bottled home. You're leaving me with their tattoos. There goes an anchor and I'm going on account. I might drift away and end up grogged. I might end up in Harlem or Long Island City. Or Wisconsin or Tai Chung. Boats and boats and garbage islands.

I don't know my way back home. Home is leaving. You are leaving me to fight Los Angeles or Pakistan. You are accidentally lost. Though I found you, you can't recognize me. Just when I called this home, you dunked back under. Just today someone scratched *I love you* in cloud letters over Lower Manhattan. Just now, yes, someone has written in the luminous sky, I love you, and you are *leaving.*

ACKNOWLEDGEMENTS & THANKS

"The Nature of Judgment" was first published in *Barrow Street* in 2011.

"Ministering a Flood (Update with God I)" and "Ministering a Tornado (Update with God II)" were first published in *Barrow Street* in December 2007.

"A Pure Subjective Commitment is Possible" and "Insubstantial Stuff of Pure Being" were first published in *The Iowa Review* in December 2007.

"Being Transformed into a Phoenix," "Enough," and "Parking Lot at Whole Foods" were first published in Heavy Feather Volume Seven, Fall 2017.

Many of these poems were written during the political sea-change of the 2016 US election and 2017 inauguration. This book is dedicated to the scholar of dictatorships, Zilahy Péter, who I first met via the Brown Foundation Fellowship Program Director Gwen Strauss at the Dora Maar House; the first three lines of the poem "Email" are from him. I want to give my deep gratitude to my writing compatriots and teachers Patricia Carlin, Joy Katz, Leah Umansky, Sophie Cooke, Kevin Young, Rosie Moffett, Brendan Kennelly, Matthew Dickman, and Eugene Ostashevsky. Thanks to Danielle Taylor for the details. To my friends, family, and colleagues who not only put up with my mad interdisciplinarity but celebrate it: Thanks, Merci, & Much Gratitude.

ABOUT ATMOSPHERE PRESS

Atmosphere Press is an independent full-service publisher for books in genres ranging from non-fiction to fiction to poetry, with a special emphasis on being an author-friendly approach to the often-brutal challenges of getting a book into the world. Learn more about what we do at Atmosphere's website, atmospherepress.com.

And of course, we encourage you to check out some of Atmosphere's latest releases, which are available at Amazon.com, BarnesandNoble.com, and via order from your local bookstore:

What Outlives Us, by Larry Levy

What I Cannot Abandon, poems by William Guest

That Beautiful Season, a novel by Sandra Fox Murphy

All the Dead Are Holy, poems by Larry Levy

Such a Nice Girl, a novel by Carol St. John

Surviving Mother, a novella by Gwen Head

How Not to Sell, by Rashad Daoudi

Rescripting the Workplace, nonfiction by Pam Boyd

Winter Park, a novel by Graham Guest

ABOUT THE AUTHOR

Mary Flanagan has written or edited five books and writes across genres including essays, poetry, fiction, and opinion pieces for *USA Today, Huffington Post, The San Francisco Chronicle*, and more. Her book *Critical Play* is essential standard-issue reading for those interested in, or studying, computer games. Her poetry has appeared in journals such as *The Iowa Review, Barrow Street, The Pinch*, and *FENCE*. She has garnered numerous accolades and awards including an honorary degree in Design from Illinois Tech, and has been a Brown Foundation fellow, an ACLS fellow, and a fellow at the MacDowell Colony, as well as a distinguished scholar at Cornell and the University of Toronto. She was recently a Museum Scholar at the Getty Museum in Los Angeles. She has exhibited artwork at the Whitney Museum of American Art, The Guggenheim, and ZKM Germany. She is also the Sherman Fairchild Professor of Digital Humanities at Dartmouth College.

Find her online at http://www.maryflanagan.com and on twitter @criticalplay.

CPSIA information can be obtained
at www.ICGtesting.com
Printed in the USA
LVOW12s2005021217
558425LV00001B/99/P